In Ruins

IN RUINS

The Once Great Houses of Ireland

PHOTOGRAPHS BY SIMON MARSDEN

TEXT BY DUNCAN MCLAREN

A Bulfinch Press Book

LITTLE, BROWN AND COMPANY

Boston • New York • Toronto • London

First United States Revised Edition
Originally published in the United States of America in 1980 by Alfred A. Knopf Inc.
This revised edition first published in Great Britain in 1997
by Little, Brown and Company (UK)

Extract from "Meditation in Time of War", taken from *The Collected Poems of W. B. Yeats*
reprinted with the permission of Simon & Schuster from *The Poems of W.B. Yeats: A New Edition*
edited by Richard J. Finneran, copyright © 1924 by Macmillan Publishing Company, renewed
1952 by Bertha Georgie Yeats. Extract from "The Curse of Cromwell" reprinted with the
permission of Simon & Schuster from *The Poems of W.B. Yeats: A New Edition* copyright © 1940
Georgie Yeats, renewed in 1968 by Bertha Georgie Yeats, Michael Butler Yeats and Anne Yeats.

ISBN 0-8212-2356-9
Library of Congress Catalog Card Number 96-85625
Bulfinch Press is an imprint and trademark of
Little, Brown and Company (Inc.)

Designed by Andrew Barron and Collis Clements Associates

Published simultaneously in Canada by
Little, Brown & Company (Canada) Limited

PRINTED IN ITALY

Half-title page: The remaining arch, Ardfert House, County Kerry.
Title page: Duckett's Grove, County Carlow.

This book is dedicated to the leprechauns

I came on a great house in the middle of the night,
Its open lighted doorway and its windows all alight,
And all my friends were there and made me welcome too;
But I woke in an old ruin that the winds howled through;
And when I pay attention I must out and walk
Among the dogs and horses that understand my talk.
O what of that, O what of that,
What is there left to say?

From 'The Curse of Cromwell', W. B. Yeats

DROMORE CASTLE

CONTENTS

What is it that people feel now when they think of Ireland? Swirling mists, mountains, shamrock and tales of magic, conquering armies of England from Edward I to Cromwell and troubles through to Churchill and on. Loyalty, politics and progress; or is it sadness, death, fever and starvation? For me it is the combination of all these things, for however cruel its beauty, the island draws, like a spell. It is a tough, hard land that takes and takes again, and gives a mixture of beauty, cruelty, unsurpassing grandness of spirit and the determination to survive.

Ireland's often tragic and troubled history together with its deep religious and mythological beliefs have combined to produce an atmosphere of remoteness and unreality among its people and their environment. This fatalistic emotion is somehow enhanced by the many decaying ruins that permeate the countryside. Many of these houses were built by all-powerful landlords, who in turn employed some of the finest architects of their age. Some were the principal seats of great families; others, used only as summer retreats, were scarcely visited. The reasons for their demise are many: Cromwell, civil wars, famine, land acts and private bankruptcy. Now time has turned full circle and they remain merely as symbols of authority and supposition.

The locations in the book cover a wide spectrum of architecture, from castles and fortified houses to abbeys and great Gothic and Palladian mansions – each in its own way resigned to an inevitable destiny. Their architectural merits have been well covered in other works. We are more interested in restoring them to their former lives.

I first visited Ireland in the summer of 1959. I was then fifteen. It was a very hot summer and we went as a family to Cork, then up to Connemara to stay in a fishing hotel once belonging to the Maharajah of Navanagar, an area north of Bombay. The water was very low and there were no fish. We stayed in a strange Georgian house that had been Victorianized, not very well. Afterwards we passed the castle of Lismore, the Irish seat of the Duke of Devonshire, one the best landlords of Ireland. Everywhere there were ruined castles, lakes and the purple hills of the west. From then on for me there were few years that did not include Ireland, with all the interest of new associations and the amusement of the races, dances and hangovers.

After a bad car accident over a weekend that included the Irish Derby, I spent more time there than usual. Later,

BALLYNALACKAN CASTLE, COUNTY CLARE

during a stay near Kilmallock, County Limerick, Mrs Dermot McCalmont told me the story of '"I doubt it," said Croker' (see page 66). A year or so later, as I was working in Ireland, I passed the strange ruins of the Croker properties and became more and more intrigued by the leftover ruins of another age. What other stories did they tell? Who had lived there? And why had they been abandoned?

In London I met by chance Simon Marsden, whose photographs revealed these gaunt and very romantic remains the way I had always wanted to see them. In his photographs I saw a special tragedy, a silence, a largeness of feeling equal to the magic of the ruins and to the people whose lives were so closely intertwined in their mystery.

Yet when asked, most Irish were simply not interested in the old buildings; they were just 'them old stones'. Even when a castle like Castle Strange was in their farmyard, the owners knew nothing of its name or past. It was just bricks and mortar, something in the way, something from their grandparents – from the troubled times or a tragedy before then, from the time when poverty was the single most important factor in their ancestors' lives. So it's not

surprising that no one wanted these walls of memories around. The sooner they go, the better. And they will go. Nature, vandalism and neglect will erode them for ever.

I wanted to reverse that and to capture these structures. The stories – now mostly hearsay – of these houses and of the people who lived in them explain many centuries.

Ireland's beauty has been called tragic, more so, I think than that of almost any other country in Europe. So restless, headstrong and ideological is the race that nothing of Ireland's past or future will ever be anything but unresolved.

> *So much time involved*
> *So little time in thought,*
> *For what might have been saved*
> *For what could have been preserved*
> *Who knows the cost?*
> *Who kept the tally?*

And so, for various reasons, a house is abandoned or burnt down and the inhabitants move away. The land is taken over, as often as not by the farm bailiffs of the old owners, as in the case of Wilton Castle where they live in the stable block of the great house. The parks have been ploughed up, gardens have disappeared and the prime trees felled for sale. Often the shell of the house remains, surrounded by a barbed wire fence to keep away the likes of Simon and myself – or to keep in cows and sheep. Signs say: 'Beware of Dogs', 'Bulls', or just the name of the owners, looming large.

Council houses encroach and take over; Kenure Park disappears under them. Leap Castle is bought by an Australian, a relation of the original family, but its condition doesn't change. Frenchpark House was torn down in 1953 because the taxes could not be paid.

But a fortunate few – the grounds of Woodstock, the St Leger House in Doneraile – are saved. Portumna stands majestic again, if roofless. Others, like Castle Lyons, glare defiantly at their noisy neighbours; a garage extends across the courtyard.

Here, then, are just a few of their stories and their images. These castles, mansions, houses – their past is Ireland, a privileged world. Their future is perhaps for the restorers, the bulldozers . . . or just indifference.
DUNCAN McLAREN, 1980.

A Note from 1995
I went to Lacken Bay, and walked up the drive from the gate to the castle. The day was bright with sunshine and the gulls swooped and cried around me before they circled and returned to the beach. The beauty of Mayo is blinding. Lacken's walls stood, but just. A lot had fallen in the years. I walked through the walls and looked out of a large bay window at the stretch of grass, to the turreted sham walls of the garden's perimeters. Several brown and white heifers joined me to observe as well. Horseflies strolled about their backs. The sun made the view shimmer. The towers divided the view, and beyond were the hills of Mayo. The park was treeless. The stable yard was full of bramble, ragwort, thyme, ivy and mud. There is such a beauty in ruins, such a stillness, and magic for the imagination. It is as if to view a great painting that the artist has had the wit only to sketch.

The same love again with the purple hills and castles of long ago. Now it was 1995. I walked back down the drive to the beach, the waves breaking as I walked across to the headland. Looking back at Lacken, all looked perfect. It could have been 1915, but it wasn't.

CADAVER, BEAULIEU HOUSE, COUNTY LOUTH

'When we were children we would dare each other to climb over the high walls that surrounded the estate, and then creep up the drive, hiding behind the massive oak trees that lined either side, until we caught sight of the baronial towers of the castle in the distance. Once we were caught by one of the many gardeners and dragged up to the mansion. I can remember standing in the vast, dark hall with my little sister, surrounded by suits of armour and tall portraits of grand people. His lordship slowly descended the great stairs and, towering above us, threatened, "Don't ever let me catch you on my land again."'

The old Irishman's lined face bore an expression of incredulity as he added, 'What do you think he meant by *his* land?'

It was a summer's evening in 1976 and I was sitting in the once-ornate lodge at the entrance to a spectacular ruined mansion in the very heart of Ireland. The room was dark and sparsely furnished, with an abundance of religious artefacts eerily lit by candlelight. I was listening to the childhood memories of an old Irish couple, now in their nineties, who in their youth had been employed on the estate during the days of Anglo-Irish ascendancy, and who later witnessed its decline and fall during the Civil War of the 1920s and the subsequent eviction of the landlord. The demesne was divided among the local people, and they had been granted this house and a few acres of land. Now, some sixteen years after the first publication of *In Ruins*, the memory of this conversation still haunts me.

One of the oldest civilizations in Europe, Ireland's cultural heritage lies deep within its Celtic traditions of myth and magic. As a race they embraced the awesome power of Nature and the suspension of reality, made poets their kings and believed in an 'other' world that lay close to the borders of the manifest, 'real' world. This 'other' world was the source of their wisdom. Being close to Nature made them close to God.

Medieval fortresses were once scattered over the land, the domain of ancient kings, built on prehistoric *ráths* or hillforts, and around whose ruins one now senses a mystical aura that emanates from the land itself, from the hills, the loughs, the rivers and the ancient gnarled trees. Many were dismantled by the British who used their great stones to build mansions, and the Gaelic chieftains were often banished overseas. But memories live on, for Ireland is in so many ways bound to its past, a country that sees progress as a return, not an outward, journey.

The Anglo-Norman invaders of the twelfth century dismissed the Irish as savage and naïve. So too did their followers, the conquering armies of Elizabeth I in the sixteenth century, and the marauding Protestant troops of Cromwell a century later. How could these intruders ever be anything other than strangers when the English obsession with formality and materialism was in direct opposition to the rampant Irish spirit, so forcefully portrayed in the wildness of their music and the imagination of their poetry? And yet the English soldiers, awarded with great estates for their loyalty to the Crown, gradually became seduced by the freedom and timelessness of this mercurial land. Everything they had known and held dear was eroded by an unstructured, alien logic until they began to lose their heads to their hearts.

Among these ruling dynasties were both good and bad landlords. Some became supporters of the Nationalist cause and were respected by their tenants and the Irish people. Others were appreciated for their charitable works, especially during the years of the Great Famine in the middle of the nineteenth century. But many who remained loyal to the Crown set themselves apart from their adopted country, and saw Ireland merely as a route to making money and furthering their political careers.

As the nineteenth century drew to a close it became clear that this privileged world was dying. The dynasties, who had relied too heavily on the glories of their ancestors, persisting with their unshakeable Victorian values and endless house parties, were doomed. As the grandeur of their mansions began to fade, they became wonderfully eccentric, moving from room to room to avoid the encroaching damp and decay, and selling their family heirlooms until all that remained were memories. Daisy Rolleston of Franckfort Castle in Tipperary was said to have given away her favourite pearl necklace to a friend, 'lest the rats should eat it', and the twice-widowed Mrs de Sales La Terriere, who often dressed as a man, was nursed in her old age by the tinkers as her castle crumbled around her. Others turned to drink and gambling, while some went quietly insane, until at last in the 1920s the Civil War finally put paid to their heritage through burnings and evictions. It was as if a supernatural power had taken revenge on this once-invincible ruling class.

When I first met Duncan we discovered that we shared a love of symbolist paintings and the mystery of ruins. He knew Ireland well and suggested we create a photographic essay on these great houses and castles. Other books have been published on the Anglo-Irish families, their homes and their achievements, but we wanted to know how and why so many of these buildings now lie in ruins.

The stories that accompany these images are a mixture of history, legend and hearsay, for this is Ireland, with its longstanding oral tradition, and more prosaically, where the burning of the Four Courts in Dublin during the Civil War destroyed many important historical records, wills and deeds.

Ireland is a country on the edge, both geographically and mentally, and such a remoteness from mainstream life creates a certain sadness. But I found nothing depressing in these ruins, only peace, for they are symbols of a vast stillness, a silence more powerful and lasting than man. Yes, it may appear arrogant for the English to expect the Irish to revere and preserve these obvious symbols of British oppression, but are they not now Ireland's heritage too?

For one throb of the artery,
While on that old grey stone I sat
Under the old wind-broken tree
I knew that One is animate
Mankind inanimate fantasy.

(From 'A Meditation in Time of War' by W. B. Yeats)

As I left the old couple and the lodge, I passed through the crumbling entrance gates, their faceless stone sphinxes still standing guard. The drive was now overgrown with brambles and scarred with potholes. I felt I was entering another world as a great silence descended. In the distance the sun was setting above an ancient hill where Druids once worshipped. Beams of light cascaded through the skeletal branches of the oak trees as all sense of reality gradually disappeared. This had once been the demesne of an Irish chieftain, the massive stones of his castle long ago embedded in the foundations of the Gothic mansion.
As I approached the ivy-clad portico of the great house, it had seemed as if time stood still, that the veil between this world and the next was transparent. These are echoes from a lost world and are at the very heart of Ireland's being.
SIMON MARSDEN, 1996

DUCKETT'S GROVE

Carlow, County Carlow.
Built in 1830. Accidentally burnt in 1933.

'Hanging in the portico was something in the style of a glass chandelier which tinkled and sounded like fairy music when the hall door was opened . . . Carved heads both human and animal adorned the outside walls,' wrote Mary Pender in the *Journal of the Old Carlow Society*, 1974, describing the former splendour of the Gothic fantasy of Duckett's Grove. It was built in 1830 by William Duckett in an estate covering more than 5,000 acres, at its entrance the most stupendous castellated gateway in southern Ireland.

The Ducketts were Quakers, originally from Lincolnshire, whose early ancestor had come to Ireland in 1641 as a bugler in Cromwell's army. Succeeding generations secured their domain through mortgages and evictions, and even had their own private burial ground, known as the Frolic, on a hill to the east of the estate. Many members of this privileged family still lie behind its high walls.

During the Troubles, the mansion was occupied by soldiers from the Irish Republican Army and many Nationalist leaders sought refuge here. The last male heir had died in 1908 but his redoubtable widow

lived on in the house until
1912, when she left for
Dublin, taking some of the
furniture and antiques with
her. The remaining contents
were sold at auction in 1929
and the land divided among

the neighbouring people, many of them descendants of the original
owners who had been evicted from their smallholdings. The collection
of fine travelling coaches was bought by a firm of undertakers and the
magnificent organ went to the church in Graiguecullen.

The Duckett ascendancy was over, and the house was
mysteriously burnt in 1933. It is now owned by a Mrs Frances Brady
who lives in one of the towers, while animals graze peacefully among
the crumbling statues.

DANGANBRACK TOWER
Quin, County Clare.
Built in the 13th century.
Destroyed by Cromwellian troops in 1640.

Ruined gables reach out towards the sky from the ancient castle of the Macnamaras. The massive, lone tower, reached by crossing a wooden bridge over a deep stream, is known as the 'ill-fated tower of Mahon Macchuin'. Here Cromwell's murderous troops spent time eating and drinking before the night sacking of Quin Abbey.

CASTLE BERNARD

Bandon, County Cork.
Built in the 17th century, remodelled in the 19th.
Burnt during the Troubles in 1921.

Just after dawn on 21 June 1921, the Earl and Countess of Bandon were surprised by intruders. Together with their house guests they were ordered out of their home and forced to watch from the lawns as it was put to the torch by the Republican Army. As her castle and its magnificent contents disappeared in a sea of flames, the countess sang 'God save the King'. She stood erect, and she sang for a long time.

The fourth earl, as Lord Lieutenant, had been a marked man for some time, and was kidnapped by the Nationalists. He was moved from place to place in the dead of night in an old wooden cart, its rough sides cutting his flesh to the bone. The seventy-year-old aristocrat claimed otherwise to have been well treated by his captors, but despite being given ample supplies of brandy, he was returned to the gutted ruin three weeks later a broken man. He died in 1924. Castle Bernard was one of sixteen country houses burnt to the ground in the Bandon area in a tragic ten-day period that deeply shocked the ruling British.

Built around an ancient fortress of the O'Mahoneys, the castle had gained a reputation as one of the happiest and most hospitable houses in Ireland, especially after the marriage of the fourth earl in 1876 to 'Doty', as she was known to her family and friends. The earl was said to have been a compulsive gambler, who sold many old masters from the family collection to pay his debts, replacing them with copies to disguise the loss. Their house parties became legendary, their larger-than-life presence earning them the nicknames King and Queen.

The fifth and last earl, known as the Earl of Abandoned, lived in a small cottage in the grounds. He died in 1979, and his title perished with him. Now the rambling, ivy-covered shell of the castle has become the refuge of owls, bats and other creatures of the night, who at the twilight hour quietly glide through the great Gothic windows as darkness and silence envelop the ruin.

Rosscarberry, County Cork.
Built in 1780. Sold in the 1920s.
Dismantled in 1952.

The vast castellated ruin stands on a hill overlooking the sea.
The original castle, known as Rathbarry, belonged to the
powerful Barry family (see Castle Lyons, page 30), but was bought by
the Frekes in the seventeenth century. By the late eighteenth century
Sir John Evans-Freke found it so dilapidated that he abandoned it
to build a grander mansion, more suited to his position in society.

In 1910 the classical interiors of the house were gutted by fire, but
restored in time for a great ball to celebrate the coming of age of the
tenth Lord Carberry in 1913. John Carberry had succeeded to the title
at the age of six, his father having died of tuberculosis at a young age.
His English mother wrote romantic novels about the Irish and raised
a dashing, reckless and, some said, sinister son, who two months after
this great party married an outstandingly beautiful English girl, in
a wedding that was to occupy the gossip columns of the newspapers
for weeks to come.

Among Lord Carberry's many exploits was learning to fly, and
he gave impromptu displays in his private plane above the castle
grounds. He went on to become an ace pilot during the Great War,
only to return to a changed world, where his previously privileged
existence was no more. He was forced to sell the great house in the
1920s. Now the spectacular view of the wild coastline from the highest
tower is intruded upon by a modern caravan site.

CASTLE LYONS

Castlelyons, County Cork.
Built in the 16th century. Accidentally burnt in 1771.

The Barrymores are remembered as, if not the most powerful, then certainly the most infamous aristocratic family in all Ireland. Of Anglo-Norman ancestry, at the height of their powers they ruled over more than 300,000 acres in County Cork from their principal seat at Castlelyons. The castle stands today as a sensational ruin, a landmark for miles around and a poignant memorial to the family's ignoble record of treachery, murder and debauchery.

The estate was originally established on the site of a fortification of the Irish clan, the O'Lehans. The Barrymores' awesome reputation was already well established by the time David Barry, who was to be created the first Earl of Barrymore in 1627, inherited the estate from a great uncle and had a magnificent mansion built for himself there.

The first earl proved as fearsome as his ancestors, but worse was to follow. The second and third earls were involved in political intrigues, and the fourth earl, who had Jacobite sympathies, was arrested for treason in 1744, betrayed by his own son and heir, who became the fifth earl. He had a weakness for drink, and he it was who began the family's descent into bankruptcy. The sixth earl, Richard Barry, who succeeded to the title in 1751 at the age of six, was a gambler and a cheat. Educated in England at Eton and Oxford, he was an absentee landlord of the worst sort. It was during his time, in 1771, that the castle was destroyed by a tragic fire.

The fire started when two itinerant tinkers, Andy Hickey and his apprentice Lewis, were repairing lead gutters on the roof. Hungry and thirsty, they

negligently left a red-hot soldering iron on woodwork when called down for food and ale. By the time they returned the roof was on fire, and they fled in fear of their lives. A crowd of villagers ran to the building to help put out the fire, but the English housekeeper, unaware of the flames and thinking them a riotous rabble, refused to let them in. The fire is said to have smouldered for three months. No trace of Hickey was ever found but Lewis settled down in Templeruane as a wigmaker, living near the graveyard and using a skull as a model. He lived to be a hundred and seventeen.

The sixth earl died at twenty-eight, and his young children were brought up in England, grossly spoiled by their guardians. Richard, the eldest, who was to become the seventh earl, inherited the family's fortune. Together with his brothers, Henry and Augustus, he became close friends with the Prince of Wales, later George IV, who dubbed the three wild characters with suitable nicknames: Richard was Hellgate, Henry, who had a club foot, was Cripplegate, and Augustus was Newgate. Their sister Caroline was known as Billingsgate, after the famous London fish market, because of her notoriously foul language. The celebrated satirical caricaturist James Gillray immortalized the three brothers as 'Les Trois Magots', and society was appalled by them. Richard died in a shooting accident at the age of twenty-four, after having squandered £300,000. Henry, the eighth and last earl, died of a fit in France in 1823.

At the Barrymore mausoleum in the gloomy, gothic graveyard of the village of Castlelyons, the iron gate has been forced open to reveal the smashed coffins of family members, their skeletons scattered over the stone floor.

Before leaving to settle a dispute with a neighbour, Sir Walter Coppinger instructed his servants that if he had not returned by a certain time from this fateful meeting, they were to set fire to his house. Sir Walter won his wager, but forgot his instructions. He drank some fine wine, arrived home late and found the house in flames.

This is one of many legends told about the infamous lord and his romantic, decaying mansion. The Coppingers were prominent merchants from the city of Cork who acquired these lands in the seventeenth century from the O'Driscolls, some say by dubious means. An ambitious tyrant, Sir Walter had planned to surround his castle with a village and convert the nearby River Roury into a canal, but these plans never came to fruition. After joining the 1641 rebellion against the British, his castle was seized and the family estates forfeited, like most of the noble Irish lords at the time.

Sir Walter was said to have had the power of life and death over the local people, and to have extended a yardarm from the gable ends of his mansion for use as a gallows. In a rage one Sunday he vowed to hang a rival. Apparently religious, he felt unable to carry out the sentence without first attending to his devotions, but as he left Mass he fell to the ground in a fit and within minutes was dead. Many saw this as an act of God, and few mourned his passing.

Another tradition states that Coppinger's Court once had golden gates that were thrown into nearby Lough Vickreen, and that if the traveller is able to line up and see through three windows of the mansion at one time, there where the sunlight falls lies Sir Walter's gold.

DONERAILE COURT

Doneraile, County Cork.
Built in 1725.
House and grounds have recently been restored
by the Irish Georgian Society.

The stately home of the St Leger family was once described as the saddest ruin in Ireland. Their ancestors had acquired the lands at Doneraile from the son of the poet Edmund Spenser in 1627. They were a great hunting family, and the first ever steeple chase took place here in 1752, from the steeple of the St Leger church to the church at nearby Buttevant.

The fourth Lord Doneraile was one of the great Victorian huntsmen. A tall and dashing figure, he seduced many young servant girls, and was cursed by an old woman whose granddaughter he had made pregnant. She prophesied that Lord Doneraile would die 'barking like a dog', and that the rooks would never rest at Doneraile until the family had gone.

Doneraile kept a pet fox, which he took with him everywhere. One day it bit him, and he was forced to travel to Paris to seek a cure for rabies from Professor Pasteur. Bored with Pasteur's strict regime, he abandoned the treatment. He died a terrible death, howling like a mad dog in one of the tiny bedrooms at the top of the house, where a groom and a gardener had to hold him down and smother him with a pillow. After his death in 1887 the family never prospered again.

Strange legends attach to the house and family. One tells of an ovoid-shaped ball of light that travels through Doneraile Park. It keeps about three feet above the ground and as it approaches it is seen to be held in the hand of a skeleton, running as fast as it can. When the seventh and last Lord Doneraile died at the rapidly fading house in 1956, the herd of deer in the park approached the building and formed a semi-circle, as if to mark the end of an epoch.

DUNBOY CASTLE

Castletownberehaven, County Cork.
Built in 1730. Altered in 1866.
Burnt during the Troubles in 1921.

In 1730 the Puxley family were granted the estates of the
O'Sullivans in west Cork, a wild, mountainous region that stood
at the very edge of the Empire. Henry and John Puxley began to
build a great mansion near the old castle of O'Sullivan Beare, and
the O'Sullivans cursed them, prophesying that cows would wander
through their halls. But the Puxleys were shrewd businessmen, and
for their own profit supported the smugglers who frequented the
untamed coastline.

In 1866 their descendant, Henry Lavallin-Puxley, began major
alterations to the estate, made possible by the great wealth the family
had accumulated after discovering copper on their lands. Tragically, his
wife died in childbirth in 1872, and after burying her in the graveyard
at Adrigole he departed for England, never to return. The great house
was left unfinished, to be used only as a summer retreat.

In 1921 Albert Thomas and his wife came as butler and cook
to Henry Puxley's grandson to prepare for an August house party.

Albert Thomas wrote in his memoirs: '. . . we found to our surprise that the castle was only half completed and the most glorious statues were unpacked, the staircase in the hall half erected . . . It seemed a pity but one must expect that sort of thing to happen over here. The air alone seemed to make one do unexpected things.'

A few weeks later the Republican Army, against the wishes of their commander, stole across the lake and burnt this wonder of the Victorian age. The Thomases had been evacuated by the British Navy a few days before to Beare Island, but saw the blaze: 'I was very sorry, sorry for all the lovely old silver, the beautiful glass and splendid linen, all being burnt, all those gorgeous statues and pictures, the wonderful drawing room, all burning – for what?' One could say for the O'Sullivans.

Dunboy and the Puxley family came to be the inspiration for Daphne du Maurier's novel, *Hungry Hill*, named after the hill that lies north-east of the castle.

MOUNT LONG CASTLE

Oysterhaven, County Cork.
Built in 1631. Burnt in 1642

In 1603 John Long, then a boy of fourteen, inherited his father's estates which included the Manor of Ringanane, and it was here in 1631 that he built the castle which now stands in ruins near the sea at Oysterhaven. The Longs were an ancient Irish family and these were part of their ancestral lands.

Ten years later, in 1641, the well-respected John Long was made High Sheriff for County Cork. In the autumn of the same year an uprising broke out against the Protestant supremacy and Long summoned his fellow Catholic rebels to a military camp which he formed on a hill at Belgooly, a few miles north of his castle. They remained at these barracks until the following spring, when Lord Baltinglass landed at Kinsale and, with his army, marched on the rebels and defeated them after a fierce battle near Bandon. Long and his sons fled, only to be captured and outlawed six months later. After the disastrous battle Long's only daughter, remembering her father's final orders, set fire to the castle to deny Cromwell his booty. The lands and ruined castle were forfeited to a Cromwellian soldier, one Giles Busteed. In 1652 Long, by then a sick man of seventy, was convicted of treason and sentenced to death along with thirty-four other rebels. They were hanged in January 1653 on Cromwell's orders.

According to the Coughlans, who now farm the land, there is an ancient burial ground not far from the ruin known as Teampuileen, an area that is shunned after dark by the superstitious locals. Some years ago a farmer tried to demolish a wall surrounding the old graveyard. He did not succeed in his act of vandalism. He saw 'something' that forced him to admit that the locals' belief in the supernatural was a great deal more than mere superstition.

KENURE PARK
Rush, County Dublin.
Built in 1703. Demolished in 1978 to make way
for the construction of council houses.

Kenure Park was built in 1703 for the second Duke of Ormonde, Viceroy of Ireland. An astute politician and a proud soldier, he was to lose his estates because of his sympathies for the Jacobite cause. The house was bought by the Palmer family, who lived here for almost two centuries before selling it in 1964. It was controversially demolished in 1978 and all that remains is the massive Corinthian portico, perhaps adding some soul to the modern housing estate that now surrounds it.

An account is told of Miss Palmer of Kenure Park, by Mr Taylor of Ardgillian Castle in 1848: 'There was such an *exposé* as poor Miss Palmer made on Friday. She was out with [Lord Donoughmores'] hounds and got 2 falls, tore all her clothes to ribbons, and remained (*à ce qu'on dit*) in her habit body and a pair of grey worsted stockings, no drawers, but the inner garments in stripes. Yet in this condition, wished to go hunting, but Lord Howth called off the hounds, and she rode home to Kenure, across the country. It is sufficiently a wayward thing for a young lady – women have no business to hunt.'

The ruin of Ardfry House stands out on a windswept peninsula of Galway Bay. It was built over an original castle of the Blake family (see Menlough Castle, page 52). Joseph Blake was created the first Earl of Wallscourt towards the end of the eighteenth century and the family continued to live here until the last owner, the second wife of the fourth Earl, gambled away their inheritance to pay off her debts in Monte Carlo. She sold the lead off every roof on the estate, including the boat house, then in desperation visited her lawyer, but collapsed in his office. She died trying to raise yet more money with which to turn the dice.

The mansion was left empty and much of the contents were stolen, though some silver was later found in a wood and the grand piano retrieved from a barber's shop. In 1922 the Wallscourt title became extinct on the death of the fifth Earl, but in 1950 the three granddaughters of the fourth Earl succeeded in legally re-claiming the house and 33 acres of their family's once large estate. The three gregarious, diminutive Blake sisters, known locally as the Three Gay Mice, now live in an outhouse close to the ruin where they are surrounded by family portraits and other memories of their illustrious past. The family's coat-of-arms, rescued from the ruin, leans against a wall of their new home. It was known as the 'Cat-a-Mountain' and the inscription reads VIRTUS SOLA NOBILITAT – Virtue Alone Enobles.

BELVIEW HOUSE
Lawrencetown, County Galway.
Built in the 18th century.
Burnt in 1922 during the Troubles.

The Gothic eye-catcher stands alone in the once beautiful, now ravaged, park of Belview House. The scant remains of the mansion are guarded by monkey-puzzle and oak trees.

The mansion and grounds were created by Walter Lawrence (1729–1796), whose ancestors came to Ireland from Lancashire in 1571. The house was burnt by the Republican Army in 1922. At the approach to the demesne is a fine triumphal arch that commemorates Henry Grattan's Ulster Volunteers (1788–9), otherwise known as the 'Irish Volunteers' – their founder had ordered them to either volunteer or be shot.

CASTLE DALY

Scalp, County Galway.
Built in the 18th century.
Abandoned in the early part of the 20th century

The one remaining façade of this eerie mansion lies perched on the side of a hill near Loughrea, like a huge raven about to flap its wings and disappear into the mercurial Irish sky. It was once one of the many homes in County Galway belonging to the powerful Daly family, whose main seat was at Raford. The Dalys, of pure Irish pedigree, were related through marriage to some of the most influential families in the west of Ireland: the Kirwans of Castle Hackett (page 54), the Brownes of the Neale (page 76), and the Burkes of Portumna (page 56).

Peter Daly had made a fortune in the West Indies when he returned to Ireland in 1820 and purchased the house from the Blake family (see Menlough Castle, page 52). It was called Gorbally Castle; he renamed it Castle Daly. According to a local man, the Daly family held many great society balls at the castle, and even now on some nights the ruined house seems to come alive again to the sounds of music and laughter.

MENLOUGH CASTLE

Galway City, County Galway.
Built in the 17th century. Accidentally burnt in 1910.

The guests would ride through the gates of Menlough Castle to the receptions of Sir John Blake, twelfth Baronet and famous spendthrift. He is said to have set forth from the small jetty in front of his home and remained adrift while furious creditors waited in vain on the lawns of the house.

The castellated Jacobean mansion, on the banks of the River Corrib, was in the possession of the Blake family from 1600 until a disastrous fire in the early part of the twentieth century. The Blakes were popular landlords. During the time of Sir Valentine, the fourteenth baronet, and Lady Blake, a great May Day regatta and tea party was held annually, to which all the local people were invited.

On the night of 26 July 1910, when Sir Valentine and Lady Blake were away in Dublin, tragedy struck. A fire broke out in the room of their invalid daughter Eleanor. She perished in the flames, and not a trace of her body was ever found. Her servant died when she jumped from a window into the courtyard below. The castle had contained many fine Elizabethan dresses and laces, much family silver and, it is said, a room completely papered in old pound notes. After the fire only one bracelet was saved. The sixteenth baronet, Sir Ulick Blake, inherited a ruin. He was found dead in his car some years ago.

'OLD' CASTLE HACKETT

Belclare, County Galway.
Built in the 13th century. Abandoned in 1705.

The ancient castle of the Kirwans lies beneath Knockmaa Hill, believed to be the legendary Otherworld seat of Finvarra, ruler of the fairies of Connaught.

> Finvarra, the king of the fairies of the West, keeps
> up friendly relations with most of the best families
> of Galway, especially the Kirwans of Castle
> Hackett, for Finvarra is a gentleman, every inch of
> him, and the Kirwans always leave out kegs of the
> best Spanish wine for him each night. In return, it
> is said, the wine vaults of Castle Hackett are never
> empty, though the wine flows freely for all comers.
>
> (Adapted from *Ancient Legends, Mystic Charms and Superstitions of Ireland*
> by the poet 'Speranza', the mother of Oscar Wilde.)

Early in the eighteenth century the Kirwans built a new mansion a short distance from the old castle, where their ancestors still reside today. In 1956 General Sir Denis Kirwan Bernard left instructions in his will that he should be buried upright in the Celtic fashion on the summit of Knockmaa Hill, facing the Galway Plain and the mountains beyond, the land that he loved.

PORTUMNA CASTLE
Portumna, County Galway.
Built in 1618. Accidentally burnt in 1826.
The castle ruin is now a National Monument.

Richard Burke, fourth Earl of Clanricarde, built this magnificent
castle overlooking Lough Derg, described as the finest and most
sophisticated house of its time in Ireland. Richard's wife was Frances
Walsingham, heiress to a large fortune through her previous marriages
to the poet and warrior Sir Philip Sydney and to the unfortunate
Earl of Essex, one-time favourite of Queen Elizabeth I.

The Irish de Burgos or Burkes derive from William de Burgo,
founder of a powerful Anglo-Norman family who came to Ireland
with Prince John in 1185. Several of Richard's fiery ancestors,
sympathetic to the Irish cause, were described by their English
contemporaries as degenerate and 'more Irish than the Irish themselves'.
Later members of the family were less popular with the locals,
however, and the house was rarely occupied. The second Marquess
of Clanricarde was a notorious absentee landlord. Enormously rich,
he was a pathological miser who lived out the final years of his life
as a recluse in London, frequently mistaken for a tramp. On his death
in 1916 the ancient Clanricarde title became extinct.

TYRONE HOUSE

Clarinbridge, County Galway.
Built in 1779. Abandoned in 1905.
Burnt in 1920 during the Troubles.

The classical mansion overlooking the sea was built for the St George family in 1779. Scion Christopher, born in 1809, was a staunch Protestant married to a Catholic woman in a union strongly disapproved of by his English contemporaries. Both of them lived to a great age, his wife living the longest. She remained in the house, along with other members of the family, in greatly reduced circumstances until her death in 1905. It is said that the cooking was done over an open fire in a room on the top floor.

The house then stood empty although the family continued to own it. Trippers came from nearby towns and villages and the caretaker allowed them to dance in the dining room. Most of the contents were sold except for an eighteenth-century marble statue of a member of the family dressed as a Roman emperor, which stood in a niche in the great hall for some twenty years after the house was abandoned. It was finally ceremoniously smashed by the people of Galway, and the house was burnt down under suspicion that it was to be used as a hospital by the Black and Tans, a force of British auxiliary soldiers that included military misfits and petty criminals.

Today a sinister, windswept ruin remains, while the St George family lies entombed in a massive Gothic mausoleum on the summit of a nearby hill.

CONOLLY'S FOLLY OR OBELISK

Castletown, Celbridge, County Kildare.
Built in 1740. Restored in the 1960s by the
Irish Georgian Society.

In 1740 Catherine Conolly, widow of William Conolly, Speaker of the Irish House of Commons and the richest man in Ireland, built a remarkable monument to his memory. It stands at the end of a two-mile vista to the north of Castletown House, the largest and, in its time, most influential eighteenth-century house in Ireland.

A juggling act of arches crowned with orbs, standing over 140 feet high, it is known as Conolly's Folly. Catherine built it to provide employment after the hardship caused by the severe winter of 1739. The wages paid were half a penny per man per day.

In March 1740 one of her disapproving family wrote: 'My sister is building an obelisk to answer a vista at the back of Castletown House; it will cost her three or four hundred pounds at least, but I believe more — I really wonder how she can do so much, and live as she does.'

Anglo-Norman Geoffrey de Maurisco founded the priory and medieval town of Kells in 1193. The many churches and castles once covered over ten acres. After the fall of the Maurisco family, the priory passed through several hands until its dissolution by Cromwell in the middle of the seventeenth century.

The remains of seven castles can still be found among the now peaceful, romantic ruins. One of these, the Prior's Castle, is also known as Philip na Maoin's Castle. Philip na Maoin, or 'Philip of the Soles', was a mysterious, emaciated and eccentric cobbler, who arrived in Kells from no one knew where in about 1790. He took up residence in the castle and lived a strange, lonely existence there for many years. He was feared by the local inhabitants who believed that he conversed with the moon and had their shoes repaired by the leprechauns.

WOODSTOCK HOUSE

Inistioge, County Kilkenny.
Built in 1740. Burnt in 1922 during the Troubles.

Woodstock once contained one of the finest libraries in Ireland and the most magnificent avenue of monkey-puzzle trees in all Europe. During the Troubles the mansion was occupied by the Black and Tans and then left empty. On hearing false rumours that the British auxiliaries might return, the house was tragically burnt by a local unit of the Republican Army.

This was the seat of the Tighe family, sympathetic to the Irish cause for generations. William Tighe, who represented Inistioge in the Irish Parliament from 1797 until 1801, violently opposed the policy of union with England. Twice offered a peerage if he would support the Act, he is recorded to have 'stoutly refused the tempting bribe, preferring to take his stand with the select band of illustrious patriots, whom nothing that a corrupt government had to offer could seduce from their loyalty to, and their love of, common country'.

The poet Mary Tighe (1772–1810), the daughter-in-law of William Tighe, spent the latter years of her young life here, stricken by consumption. One morning in 1810 she walked down from the great house to the village of Inistioge below, and on her return collapsed on to a sofa and died. The sculptor Flaxman was summoned to make a cast of her reposing. He took three days to reach Woodstock, but no one moved her. The statue can be found in a small neoclassical mausoleum in the Protestant churchyard at Inistioge, and her fragile ghost has been seen retracing the steps of her last fateful walk, as graceful in death as in life.

Here too lived the legendary figure of Lady Louisa Tighe. On the eve of Waterloo, a child of twelve, she helped her godfather to buckle on his sword. Her godfather was Ireland's greatest soldier, the Iron Duke of Wellington.

Ballynaguarde was built in 1774 by the powerful and notorious Croker family, originally from Devon in England. The entrance was through a graceful pavilion of Grecian design, surmounted by lions and eagles, and the ornamental gardens were adorned with classical statuary.

Larger-than-life Captain Edward Croker bankrupted the estate. He was described during his lifetime as 'a worthless spendthrift who brought up an arrogant race of uneducated blockheads of both sexes', but the most famous story of his colourful life concerned his death. As he lay in bed suffering from a terminal illness, his son Robert, a clergyman, was summoned to console him and administer the last rites. At the end of his prayers Robert concluded, 'It is a far, far better place that you go to now.' Captain Croker, sitting up in bed, surveyed his wondrous demesne through the window, replied 'I doubt it', and fell back dead. The house is known locally as 'I-doubt-it Hall'.

CARRIOGUNELL CASTLE
Clarina, County Limerick.
Built in the 15th century. Blown up in 1691.

Standing on a craggy rock, high above the Shannon estuary, this was once a stronghold of the mighty O'Brien clan. A landmark for miles around, its shattered keep and ivy-clad ramparts are scarred and mutilated by violence and war. After a ferocious siege in 1536 the castle fell to Lord Deputy Grey, who subsequently hanged the entire garrison. The fortress was destroyed in 1691 after surrendering to the Williamites during the siege of Limerick.

The rock on which the castle stands is known as 'Carekogunyel' – the Rock of the Candle. Legend tells of an evil witch who lit a candle each evening on the rock, whose light after nightfall slew all that saw it. A warrior of the legendary strongman Finn mac Cool, protected by an enchanted cap, scaled the rock and hurled the sorceress's candle into the Shannon.

DROMORE CASTLE

Pallaskenry, County Limerick.
Built between 1867 and 1870. Abandoned in 1950.
Now under restoration.

In the first half of the nineteenth century the Earls of Limerick lived in England, but when the young and imaginative third earl succeeded to the title he decided to build a spectacular castle on his Irish lands. He commissioned Edward William Godwin, the innovative and daring Victorian architect, to create his fantasy.

Godwin, an aesthete and friend of Oscar Wilde, was inspired to model the castle on its medieval predecessors, incorporating the popular Gothic Revival style of the time. The centrepiece was to be a great Round Tower based on Cormac's Chapel, the magnificent ecclesiastical ruin on the Rock of Cashel. The interiors of the mansion were furnished in an affected style that Godwin's friends said was influenced by his mistress, the English actress and singer Ellen Terry.

The fortified appearance of the castle suggested it expected trouble. Indeed, the Limericks had been unpopular landlords. However the mansion had been built in great haste, and its eventual downfall was not violence, but damp. Today the ruin is silhouetted against the skyline, as mysterious and enchanting as any fairytale.

Godwin is said to have remarked to a group of architects, 'If you receive an Irish commission, refuse it.' His other failure was Glenbeigh Towers, County Kerry – damp again. Furniture from Dromore, designed by Godwin, has come to the surface in various auctions over the last decades, and has been found in the most unlikely places, including the local inn and the butcher's shop.

MOUNTSHANNON

Castleconnell, County Limerick.
Built in the 18th century. Burnt in 1920
during the Troubles.

The Mountshannon estate once covered over 900 acres, half of it parklands and gardens. Its most famous owners were the Fitzgibbons, whom legend has it rose to prominence after marrying into fairy gold. Infamous 'Black Jack' Fitzgibbon, born in 1748, was Lord Chancellor of Ireland and one of the most powerful men of his day. Notorious as an opponent of Catholic emancipation, his favourite expression was that he would make the Irish 'as tame as a mutilated cat'. He was created Earl of Clare in 1795, and when he first appeared in the English House of Lords William Pitt said, 'Good God, did you ever hear in all your life such a rascal?' When he died in 1802 dead cats were hurled upon his coffin by the people of Dublin.

The second Earl of Clare was rumouredly castrated in a Turkish brothel while on a escapade with his friend, the poet Lord Byron, and died in 1851 without issue. The title passed to his brother Richard, whose only son, Viscount Fitzgibbon, was killed at the Charge of the Light Brigade during the Crimean War. A statue of him was erected at Sarsfield Bridge, but was blown up during the Troubles. His ghost, appearing to his regiment in India, inspired a Kipling short story.

The last member of the family to own the house was Lady Louisa Fitzgibbon, Richard's daughter. A giver of lavish banquets and balls, she exhausted the estate's money. Expecting it to solve her financial problems, she became engaged to a Sicilian nobleman. Alas he too was penniless, and marrying her for the same reason. During a celebratory party, the bailiff's agents arrived to evict her, and drew the final curtain on her family's idiosyncratic reign.

MANISTERNAGALLIAGHDUFF OR 'OLD ABBEY'

Shanagolden, County Limerick.
Founded in the 13th century. Dissolved in 1541.

The once extensive grounds of St Katherine's nunnery are now enveloped by dense undergrowth and ancient twisted trees, and an uneasy silence has descended on the ruins. According to the historian John Wardell, writing in the *Irish Archaeological Journal* in 1904, little is known of the medieval Augustinian nunnery, despite its considerable size and importance. No records exist of its foundation, but it is first mentioned in the Inquisition of 1298.

In 1541, the nunnery was dissolved by the Pope, after, it is said, an abbess had shocked and terrified the people of the county with her sexual exploits and her practices in the 'black arts'. After the departure of the other nuns, the abbess remained in the deserted convent,

attaining such an age that her face became 'quite black'. She hid away in the sacristy and died alone in the room that became known as the Black Hag's Cell.

Many legends attach themselves to the nunnery. One of these concerns an Earl of Desmond and his countess, who, during one of the many battles waged between the Geraldines and the Butlers, escaped from their besieged castle. During the escape, the countess was mortally wounded. Her heartbroken husband brought her body to the deserted nunnery and hastily made her a grave under the altar in the main chapel. He travelled on, never knowing that he had buried his countess alive. Her ghost still haunts the scene of her horrific death.

The Browne family were among the first English settlers in this part of the country, at the time of Elizabeth I. Sir John Browne became the first Lord Kilmaine in 1789. Their great house has gone, but within its peaceful demesne several mysterious follies remain.

Close to the road is a stepped pyramid, designed for the first Lord Kilmaine and allegedly built over an ancient cairn. The nine tiers were once crowned with a lead statue of Apollo.

Deeper within the park stands the classical Temple of the Winds, now a refuge for wild animals. Stranger still is the curious monument known as the Gods of the Neale: these ancient sculpted figures of pagan gods were believed to have been worshipped by Edda and Con, legendary founders of Connaught. Whether it is a folly, is not known.

Nearby is the melancholy ruin of the Protestant church. From its tall tower the great bell was said to ring of its own accord when a member of the Browne family died. The fifth Lord Kilmaine, who sold the house to a tenant in 1925, later shot himself when seduced by alcohol and short of money.

ARCH HALL

Wilkinstown, County Meath.
Built in the 18th century. Burnt in 1922
during the Troubles.

The present owner of the ruin of Arch Hall, Mrs Kitty Colwell, lives in a farmhouse close by. She has heard many stories of the house's strange past. One of the rooms in the mansion before it was destroyed is reputed to have been entirely gold, from the paint on the walls to the furniture and the picture frames. Another story tells of a young house guest of the Garnetts who saw an unfamiliar man and woman descend the main stairs, arm in arm, dressed in evening dress. She told her hosts that she had not known they had other house guests. 'Oh, we don't,' they replied. 'Those are just our friends from the past.'

An impressive pedimented arch in the grounds gave the hall
its name. Either side of the arch were planted two Chilean pine trees
to celebrate the birth of twin boys to the Garnett family in the early
1900s. One of the trees survives in memory of a life given during
World War I. The other has withered, for the second son returned
from the war deranged from the horrors he had seen. Later the boys'
father, returning home from lengthy travels, went blind and died from
a mysterious illness after stealing the eye of an Indian god from
a roadside shrine.

LEAP CASTLE
Aghancon, County Offaly.
Built during the 14th century.
Ransacked and burnt in 1922 during the Troubles.

The original tower house of Leap Castle was the principal seat of the powerful and warlike O'Carrolls. It stood on a vast, ancient rock guarding a strategic pass through the wild Slieve Bloom mountains. The O'Carrolls were the last clan to surrender to the British in the seventeenth century. Their fearsome reputation, however, they did not surrender.

Above the main hall of the original tower is the Bloody Chapel where 'One-eyed' Tadhg O'Carroll slew his brother at the altar. Late at night passersby on the main road have seen a window of this room suddenly illuminated by a strange light. Off this haunted chamber is a spiked oubliette, a secret dungeon into which unsuspecting prisoners were thrown and conveniently forgotten. Several cartloads of human and animal bones were removed from here in the late nineteenth century, and the last use of the murder hole was dated as the seventeenth century. Below the tower stretched a network of deep dungeons hewn into rock, containing bricked-up passages and secret chambers. Several human skeletons and spearheads have been found here too.

In 1599 Sir Charles Carroll, the last ruling chieftain, hired a force of MacMahons of Monaghan as mercenaries against the rebel Earl of Tyrone. Either fearing treachery, or unwilling to pay them their dues, he got them drunk at a lavish feast and had them massacred in their sleep.

The Darby family from Leicestershire in England acquired the estate in the seventeenth century when Jonathan Darby married the same Sir Charles's daughter. A staunch Royalist, and known as the Wild

Captain, he was said to have hidden a fabulous hoard of treasure in the grounds of the castle with the help of two servants, whom he then murdered. Imprisoned for treason and released many years later, half-mad, he couldn't remember where he had hidden the hoard. The mystery remains.

It was the Darbys who added the Gothic wings to the castle in the mid-eighteenth century. More distinguished than 'Wild Captain' Darby was Admiral Sir Henry Desterre Darby, who commanded HMS *Bellerophon* at the Battle of the Nile in 1798. His ship later carried Napoleon into exile. The Darbys could not shake off their castle's ghoulish reputation, however. Overnight guests were frequently faced with the terrifying spectre of a tall, female figure in a red gown, a hand raised menacingly high clutching a radiant dagger.

The strangest and most demonic apparition in the ancient buildings is a foul-smelling, elemental, half-human half-beast that haunts the ancient stairway overlooking the Hangman's Field below. He is said to embody all the horrific deeds that have taken place at the castle through the centuries.

The Darby's tenuous occupation ended when the castle was burnt by members of the Republican Army in 1922, while the family were living in England. A mob looted and ransacked the mansion and hanged the tame peacocks from the battlements. Now only the troubled spirits from the past, and the endlessly circling crows, guard these forgotten towers.

RATHMORE CASTLE

Sharavogue, County Offaly.
Built in the 15th century. Destroyed in the 17th century.

Tadhg O'Carroll of Rathmore was one of the principal officers who led the Catholic siege of Birr in 1643, and a well-known rebel. Unwilling to submit to the British, he was dispossessed in 1652, and died a few years later. In 1661 his widow Margaret successfully petitioned the Crown to have the lands restored to herself and her two sons.

Little now remains of the castle, built on the site of an ancient *ráth*. An old woman, herding cows, talked about the castle's history: 'It was once the fortress of the legendary Tadhg O'Carroll, with four mighty towers that covered two acres of land, but nature has taken it for herself now.'

Built around an original tower house, this tall crumbling mansion, with its four massive chimneys and eyeless windows, was once the seat of the L'Estrange family from Norfolk. Their coat-of-arms on the ruined stable is now almost completely covered by creeping ivy, but one can still make out the inscription: 'NEC TEMERE NEC TIMIDE' — Neither Reckless Nor Timid.

By the side of the entrance drive, beneath an ancient oak tree, lies a round ornamental stone covered with enigmatic spiral decorations. This ancient stone once played an important part in Celtic rituals that we can no longer know anything of. An old man approached. He had lived here all his life, but showed little interest in the history of the ruin; indeed, did not even call it Castle Strange but simply the 'old castle'. As he walked away, he muttered beneath his breath: 'Castle Strange, what an odd name to be calling a castle now.'

Almost nothing remains of the great Palladian mansion of the Lords de Freyne, sold by the seventh Lord de Freyne in 1953 and demolished shortly after to avoid a roof tax. John French built it in 1729, and his son Arthur, the fourth Lord de Freyne, inherited a substantial fortune. When Arthur died in 1769, his wake was a three-day extravaganza, and the gentry of the county feasted, drank and danced around his body. The fifth Lord de Freyne was less fêted. His effigy was hanged in Frenchpark village by the local Irish during the Great Famine in the nineteenth century.

All that now remains of the once-prosperous domain are an ivy-clad brew-house, the petrified lake and a souterrain. The man who tends this park, whose father tended it before him, said: 'It was a beautiful house. I'm sorry you hadn't more to see.'

SEAFIELD HOUSE
Coolera, County Sligo.
Built in 1840. Abandoned in 1940.

William Phibbs was a man of considerable wealth, and it was his intention that his new family seat at Seafield House would reflect his family's opulence, and rival, if not surpass, the other great houses of the county.

His eldest son, Owen, succeeded him in 1881, forty years after the great house was built. He was considered a benevolent landlord – though tenants were obliged to salute him as he drove past in his carriage. Owen Phibbs's work as an archaeologist in Egypt and Syria furnished him with a booty of swords, daggers and mummies. Soon after installing it at the house, a malicious poltergeist started work, smashing crockery and ornaments through the night. Many servants left, and an old gardener was terrified by a tall, dark apparition that disappeared into the nearby sea with an echo of maniacal laughter. In 1899 Owen Phibbs changed the name of the house to Lisheen in an attempt to fight off its reputation.

Basil Phibbs succeeded his father at Lisheen. A quiet man, he served as an ambulance driver in the French Red Cross during World War I. His son Geoffrey, in his book *The Emerald Isle*, wrote: 'Only once could he even be suspected of trying to kill anything larger than a pheasant, and that was when he fired a shot from his dressing room window towards the Republican Army on the tennis court of our own house at Lisheen. He missed the soldiers as, indeed, he missed many a pheasant.' After Basil's death in 1938 the house was sold and stripped of its contents down to the naked walls, ending the Phibbs's association with the area. Even the changed name failed to stick.

Lough Derg, County Tipperary.
Built in the 14th century. Destroyed in the 17th century.

Appearing like a ghost ship in the night, this O'Kennedy castle is said to conceal a fabulous hoard of treasure. It was hidden here by Edmond Roe O'Kennedy who, together with fellow Irishmen, rebelled against the English Queen Elizabeth in the sixteenth century, and was subsequently killed at the castle. The secret of the whereabouts of the treasure died with him. It has never been found.

BALLINAKILL CASTLE
Dunkerrin, County Tipperary.
Built in 1580. Destroyed in the 17th century.

Sheep wander through the great halls of the castle that was built in the sixteenth century by the Butlers, Earls of Ormonde, to subdue the warlike Irish clans. The Butlers (their original family name was Walter) were a Norman family who came to England with William the Conqueror in the eleventh century. In 1185 Prince John granted land in Ireland to Theobald Fitzwalter, who founded the Butlers' Irish dynasty. Much of this land was in the Irish midlands, and as the Butlers sought to secure an iron grip over the region, so they began a conflict that lasted for over five hundred years.

The Butlers' main seat was to the south of Ballinakill in the medieval city of Kilkenny. Piers Butler, eighth Earl of Ormonde, whose tomb lies in the cathedral in Kilkenny, had two elder brothers. Edmund and Theobald, however, were deemed illegitimate. Through Edmund, whose line intermarried with Irish stock, descended the ancestors of perhaps Ireland's greatest poet and staunch nationalist, William Butler Yeats.

The O'Kennedy's of Upper and Lower Ormonde struggled against the Anglo-Norman Butlers (see Ballinakill Castle, page 96) for almost five hundred years. Lackeen, probably the finest of their castles (Annagh, page 94, was another), was forfeited to the Cromwellians in 1653. John Kennedy regained possession of his family's lands in the eighteenth century and during alterations to the castle discovered an ancient, illuminated vellum manuscript, known as the Stowe Missal, that had been hidden in an ornate casket and bricked up in a wall of the fortress by one of his ancestors.

John Kennedy died in 1766 and is buried in nearby Lorrha Abbey.

THOMASTOWN CASTLE

Golden, County Tipperary.
Built in 1670. Abandoned in 1872.

The home of the Mathew family, the Earls of Llanduff, was the stage for the most extravagant entertaining in all Ireland, described by Thomas Campbell of Tyrone in 1776 'as having all the capabilities of a terrestrial paradise'. 'Grand George' Mathew, good-looking, widely travelled and an excellent swordsman, turned the Gothic pile into a free luxury hotel for his friends and, indeed, anyone who wanted to come. As they arrived at the castle he greeted them with this speech: 'This is your castle. Here you are to command as absolutely as in your own home. From this moment you are never to know me as master of the house, but only consider me as one of the guests.'

In his *Life of Dean Swift*, Thomas Sheridan described their visit. On turning into the avenue, Swift, appalled by the size of the house, promptly called on his coachman to turn about and drive back to Dublin, for he could not think of mixing with such a crowd. Sheridan prevailed on him to stay. When greeted by George Mathew, Swift replied, 'Well, then I invite you and Dr Sheridan to be my guests while I stay, for I shall hardly be tempted to mix with the mob below.' But he changed his mind and stayed for four months, a leader of the revels.

Mathew's contemporaries thought him insane, but he worked hard, rising at cockcrow and drinking little, and he husbanded his fortune so well that he left it intact for his descendants. However, his only son died before him, and his grandson a year after him in 1838. In 1841 the Llanduff title became extinct and from 1872 the castle was abandoned. In 1938 the decaying ruin was bought by the archbishop and historian, and family descendant, David Mathew, to save it from oblivion.

TIMONEY PARK
Roscrea, County Tipperary.
Built in the 19th century. Burnt in 1922
during the Troubles.

From the middle of the seventeenth century, the contrast between the lifestyles of the newly planted English 'adventurers', or 'undertakers' as the Irish preferred to call them, and those of the once powerful Gaelic warlords whose lands had  often been confiscated, was immense. On one hand were the newly built, luxurious homes of the settlers, where they entertained their fellow countrymen in lavish style. On the other were the tall, ancient tower houses with their thatched halls, where the hereditary Irish chieftains existed in much reduced circumstances, or which they had been forced to leave.

This sombre ivy-clad ruin had been the home of the Anglo-Irish Parker-Hutchinson family. It was burnt, like so many other mansions, during the Troubles. Close to the ruin are more than three hundred large stones scattered over a wide area. Whether these are a prehistoric monument, or were created as a folly, is a mystery.

This Gothic house first belonged to the Costens. A young heir of the Costens was tricked by his guardian and branded a thief. Pursued by troops along the cliffs near the house, his horse stumbled and he was hanged by his own reins at a spot still known as 'Crook-an-Heire' — the Gallows of the Heir.

The house passed through the Prendergasts to the Coghlans. Madam Coghlan supported her family's extravagant existence by helping the smugglers who frequented the coast. Her daughter Thomasina at the age of eighty-five still played with dolls and dressed like a child, and her son Jeremiah carried two kittens wherever he went. Two other children, both girls, were very beautiful. One married the French Duc de Castries, the other the eighth and last Earl of Barrymore, the notorious 'Cripplegate' (see Castle Lyons, page 30). The Coghlans, like the Barrymores, were destined to financial ruin, and by now the house was believed to be cursed and haunted. Among the many stories at this time was one of a dangerous loose step on the main staircase that would not stay in place ever since the skeleton of a child had been discovered beneath it.

The last owners of the fateful mansion were the McKennas,
who brought it from Marshall MacMahon, victor of Magenta and
president of France, and a grandson of the Duc de Castries. Sir Joseph
McKenna was a banker and politician and he and his wife hosted
many important parties here, when the avenue of pine trees from the
entrance gates up to the house would be lit by five hundred torches.

The monument that still guards the McKenna mausoleum is
now so overgrown that you could stumble upon it only by chance.
The inscription reads:

> My Life is like a broken stair,
>
> winding round a ruined tower,
>
> and leading nowhere.

KILLUA CASTLE

Clonmellon, County Westmeath.
Built in 1780. Transformed to fashionable Gothic in 1830.
Abandoned and dismantled in the 1930s.

One of the most romantic ruins in Ireland, Killua Castle was once the seat of the Chapman family, who originated from Leicestershire in England and gained prominence through the patronage of their celebrated cousin Sir Walter Ralegh. The vast demesne of lakes and follies eventually bankrupted the family, who had tried to keep up with their very wealthy neighbours. An obelisk on the land commemorates the planting of the first potato in Ireland by Ralegh. The obelisk is dated 1810; thirty years later the crop failed and the Great Famine began.

Thomas Chapman (1848–1919), the last of the line, married a Rochford who bore him four daughters. The marriage was unhappy, and he spent long periods of time in England, where he met and fell in love with Sarah Dunner, and changed his name from Chapman to Lawrence. They had five sons. One of them is known by his initials, T. E.: Lawrence of Arabia, the controversial white leader of the Arabs during World War I. An enigmatic figure, Lawrence never lived at Killua, although he visited.

Jacky Dalton, the land steward to Sir Benjamin Chapman in the late eighteenth century, remains a spirit at Killua. He had a close relationship with his employer, and would sit at the foot of Sir Benjamin's dinner table wearing a particularly strange yellow wig and playing bagpipes for guests. He is believed to have relieved his master of considerable sums of money, but after his master's death turned to drink, and finally committed suicide by jumping into a lake.

Now many of Killua's lakes are drained and the follies dismantled and sold, but the beautiful ruin remains on a hill, a monument to the extravagance of a more romantic age.

MOYDRUM CASTLE

Athlone, County Westmeath.
Built in 1814. Burnt in 1921 during the Troubles.

Sir Jonah Barrington observed that William Handcock 'made and sang songs against the Union in 1799 at a public dinner for the opposition, and made and sang songs for it in 1800. He got a peerage.' William Handcock became Lord Castlemaine in 1812, and had this fine Gothic Revivial castle built in 1814.

In July 1921 the British Army, searching for arms, burnt down three neighbouring farms, and the local Republican Army retaliated by burning down Moydrum, an obvious symbol of English oppression. Lord Castlemaine was absent. It was left to his wife and three daughters to care for the charred shell, but never again to live within its fine walls.

ROSMEAD HOUSE

Delvin, County Westmeath.

Built in the 18th century. Burnt in 1923.

The Grand Triumphal Arch of Rosmead, called 'Smiling Bess', belonged to Mr Smyth of Glananea, County Westmeath, in the late eighteenth century. He was known as Smyth With the Gates, until he gave his triumphal arch to his neighbour at Rosmead nearby, when he was renamed Smyth Without the Gates.

The arch remains the silent entry to the forgotten ruins of Rosmead House.

WATERSTON HOUSE

Athlone, County Westmeath.
Built in 1749. Abandoned in 1923.
Dismantled in 1930.

Waterston House was built in 1749 for Gustavus Handcock (see also Moydrum, page 110), an ancestor of the Harris-Temple family who were to reside here until 1923 when, through extravagance and bad management, they went bankrupt. The mansion had been surrounded by parklands adorned with monuments that included a hermitage, a spectacular pigeon house, a lake with a mock castle on an island, and a fine walled kitchen garden with an ornamental arch.

One summer's evening, an old man told me the story of the last members of the Harris-Temple family to live here. The master of the house had become blind and taken to drink, and only emerged to order a servant to walk all the way to Athlone to pick up special white powder from the apothecary. The white powder, when mixed with whisky, would make two bottles out of one. In his younger days, the man had been the host of elaborate parties, and his wife was said to have had frequent affairs with the visiting British Army officers.

In 1930, the steward, who had been partly responsible for the bad management, took possession of the house and sold much of its contents, including the doors and windows. Harris-Temple returned to England where he was knocked down in the street and killed. Some years later, in an answer to persistent rumours, the lake was drained and two human heads were discovered. In the now ravaged gardens the skeleton of another man was found, but none of these remains has ever been identified.

The present owner of the land lives in a modest bungalow close to the ruin. He has an old photograph that shows a gathering of the county's finest worthies in the 1890s, standing on the manicured lawns in front of the glittering house, confident in all their spectacular finery that their age would last for ever.

CASTLEBORO HOUSE

Enniscorthy, County Wexford.
Built in 1840. Burnt in 1923 during the Troubles.

This huge and imposing classical mansion was built in 1840 to replace an earlier house. It was in the hands of the Carew family, originally from Devon in England, who had been granted lands in the county of Wexford during the reign of Charles II. The Carews enhanced their fortunes through astute marriages and distinguished careers in politics and the law.

The first Lord Carew was a supporter of the Irish cause and opposed the Act of Union in 1801. It is said that shortly after Carew became a Member of Parliament he was visited at Castleboro by Viscount Castlereagh, whose brief it was to buy off the landlord class. He tried to bribe Carew to vote in favour, and found himself thrown out of the house.

After the death of the first Lord Carew in 1856, the family descendants spent little time at the great house, although in the summer months they would hold house parties for their English friends. On the night of 3 February 1923, during a dinner party, the house was burnt to the ground by the Republican Army. Guests standing at the foot of the great steps leading up to the mansion watched in horror as the then Lady Carew ran back up in a vain attempt to rescue her favourite heraldic needlework cushions from the the west wing before the roof collapsed. Her husband, the third Lord Carew, died two months later of a broken heart. Today the great house is a dark, empty shell.

The Carew family motto is 'Nil Admirari' — to be surprised at nothing.

COOLBAWN HOUSE
Enniscorthy, County Wexford.
Built in 1840. Burnt in 1914 during the Troubles.

It took Francis Bruen twenty-five years to build this Tudor Revival fantasy. He resided mostly in England and the estate was run in his absence by his much-hated agent Mr Routledge, who would pay the rent arrears of the Protestant tenants rather than let the land fall into the hands of the Catholics. If the Catholics could not pay, their land was given to the Protestants.

Every Friday fifty horses were shod in preparation for Mr Bruen, but he seldom, if ever, came. According to John Hennessy, son of the present local blacksmith, the end for Coolbawn came late one winter's night during the Troubles. Some family retainers were awakened and held at gunpoint by the Republican Army at a smaller house on the estate. Their commander thought the house was Coolbawn and ordered his men to set fire to it. He realized his error when he saw the unremarkable contents of the interior. So he sought out the great house and torched it.

TINTERN ABBEY
Bannow Bay, County Wexford.
Founded around 1200. Dissolved in 1538.
Presently under restoration.

Said to have been built as a result of a vow, Tintern Abbey, or 'Tintern de Voto', lies on the west shore of Bannow Bay and is perhaps the most beautiful monastic settlement in Ireland. William Mareschal, the Norman Earl of Pembroke, was trapped in a storm while crossing from Wales to Ireland: if it please God to save his life, he vowed, he would build a religious house at the place where he landed. He dedicated the abbey to the Virgin Mary and transported Cistercian monks from Tintern Abbey in his Welsh homelands to worship here.

The abbey was dissolved in 1538 and the lands granted in 1652 to an Elizabethan soldier, Sir Anthony Colclough from Staffordshire, who turned the building into a dwelling house where his descendants lived for almost four hundred years. The Colcloughs created a powerful dynasty in the region and by the end of the eighteenth century were said to own a fifth of County Wexford. Unlike many of their fellow Anglo-Irish landowners, they had in the main an exceptionally good relationship with the local people and several of their number both risked and lost their lives fighting for the Irish cause through the centuries.

One of them was Sir Caesar Colclough, who inherited the abbey in 1723. A great athlete, he held sporting galas in the grounds for his tenants with abundant free food and drink. He lived among his tenants, and they called him the 'Great Caesar'.

The family's reign ended when Miss Lucy Colclough presented the abbey to the nation in 1958.

WILTON CASTLE

Enniscorthy, County Wexford.
Built in the 19th century. Burnt in 1923
during the Troubles.

A great moat and sham fortifications still surround the once resplendent seat of the Alcock family, who were in residence here from 1695. Colonel Harry Alcock added the great towers and magnificent gardens in the nineteenth century and it seems that by all accounts the Alcocks were good landlords. But as the Civil War raged the family left Ireland for the safety of Shropshire in England in 1922, leaving the castle in the hands of the caretaker. He was to prove no match for the Republican Army, who set fire to the mansion on the evening of 5 March 1923. The intruders apologized for what they had been commanded to do.

Many supernatural stories centre on the dramatic silhouette of the castle. On the anniversary of the death of Harry Alcock, who died in 1840, a ghostly carriage is seen on the castle driveway. His ghost is also seen on the roads around the castle, and a local shoemaker claimed to have spoken with it. Another local man said that strange lights sometimes shine in a tower of the castle where an old woman, a former actress, had been burnt to death.

ACKNOWLEDGEMENTS

We would like to thank the following people for their help, information, hospitality and inspiration, as well as the many landlords, farmers, innkeepers and librarians of Ireland whose help and kindness will not be forgotten: The Three Sisters of Ardfry House, Elizabeth Lady Arnold, Princess Minnie de Beauvau Craon, Miss Frances Brady, Miss Caroline Carey, Mr Gerald Carroll, Mrs Mary Byron Casey, Miss Anne Charlton, Mr Willy Cody, Mr and Mrs John Cohane, Mr John Colclough, Mrs Kitty Colwell, M. and Madame Marcel Croes, The Earl and Countess of Dunraven, The Late Dowager Countess of Dunraven, Messrs Michael and Thomas Flahaven, Miss Fiona Ford, Mr John and Lady Jennifer Fowler, Mrs John Gallagher, Mr Thomas Garland, Mr Shaun Gaul, Mr Tom Graves, Mr Johnny Hennessey, Mr and Mrs Patrick Hennessy, Mr R. William Higgins, Mr and Mrs Christopher Hindley, Mr Thomas Kenney, Mr Johnny Keyhoe, Mr Alan and Lady Vivienne Lillingston, Mrs Donna Long, Mr and Mrs George Loudon, Mrs Simon Marsden, The Late Mrs Dermot McCalmont, Mr Michael McCalmont, Mr John McCann, Mrs Leila McGarel-Groves, Mr Matthew McNulty, Mrs Nora Moran, The Earl and Countess of Mount-Charles, Mr John Nankivell, Miss Angela Neville, Mr Nicholas Nicholson, Mr Gerard O'Brien, DLIS, Messrs Ruan and Oscar O'Lochlainn, Mr Percy Paley, The Late Col. Power, Mrs Gervas Power, Mr Piers Rogers, The Late Major and Mrs Patrick Rome, Mr Michael Rooney, The Earl and Countess of Rosse, Mr Patrick Ryan, Sergeant Scully, Father Slattery, Mr and Mrs Ian Spence, Heinrich Graf von Spreti, Mr T. Alan and The Late Mrs Staunton, Miss Jane Storr, Count Trolle-Bunde, The Old Coachman of Waterston House, and Mrs Beryl Windsor.

A special thank you to Vivien Bowler, Christian Gotsch, Andrew Barron and Mari Roberts for their invaluable help in editing, designing and producing this book.

Ancient Legends, Mystic Charms and Superstitions of Ireland, Lady Jane Wilde. London, 1888.

Burke's Guide to Country Houses, Vol.1, Ireland, Mark Bence-Jones. London, 1978.

The Castles of County Cork, James N. Healy. Cork and Dublin, 1988.

Castles of Ireland, C. L. Adams. London, 1904.

Castles of Ireland, Brian De Breffny and George Mott. London, 1977.

'The Curse of Cromwell', *The Collected Poems of William Butler Yeats*. London, 1950.

'The Empty Gardens of Ardo', *Country Life Annual*, Mark Bence-Jones. London, 1968.

The Follies and Garden Buildings of Ireland, James Howley. Yale University Press, 1993.

The Great Hunger, Cecil Woodham-Smith. Penguin Books, 1962.

Guide to Kilkenny City and County, P. M. Egan. Kilkenny, 1884.

Historical and Topographical Notes, etc. on Buttevant, Castletownroche, Doneraile, Mallow, and Places in their Vicinity, Vol.3, J. G. White. Cork, 1905–1916.

The Houses of Ireland, Brian De Breffny and Rosemary Ffolliott. London, 1975.

The Illustrated Guide to the Blackwater and Ardmore. 1840.

Illustrated Guide to the City of Limerick and Antiquities in Its Neighbourhood. Hodges, Figgins, and Co. Ltd., Limerick.

Irish Archaeological Journal, Vol.18 (5th series), 1908.

The Irish Country House – A Social History, Peter Somerville-Large. Sinclair Stevenson, 1995.

Irish Eccentrics, Peter Somerville-Large. Hamish Hamilton, 1975.

The Journal of the Cork Historical and Archaeological Society, Vols.70–71, 1965–66.

The Journal of the Galway Archaeological and Historical Society, Vol.1, no.1; Vol.2, no.1.

The Journal of the Kildare Archaeological Society, Vol.2, 1898.

The Last Earls of Barrymore, 1769-1824, John R. Robinson. London, 1894.

Limerick: Its History and Antiquities, Ecclesiastical, Civil, and Military, From the Earliest Ages, M. Lenihan. Dublin, 1884 and 1886.

Lost Demesnes, Edward Malins and The Knight of Glin. London, 1976.

North Munster Antiquarian Journal, Vols.3–5, 1942–48.

North Munster Studies, Etienne Rynne, ed. Limerick, 1967.

Old Kilkenny Review, no.4, 1951; no.21, 1969.

Picnic in a Foreign Land, Ann Morrow. Grafton Books, 1989.

Sketches in Carbery, County Cork, Daniel Donovan. Dublin, 1876.

Some Celebrated Irish Beauties of the Last Century, F. Gerard. London, 1895.

Some Georgian Houses of Limerick and Clare, S. Stewart and R. Herbert. 1949.

South Westmeath, Farm and Folk, Jeremiah Sheenan. Dublin, 1978.

Topographical Dictionary of Ireland, Vol.2, Samuel Lewis. London, 1837.

Twilight of the Ascendancy, Mark Bence-Jones. Constable & Co., 1987.

Wait and See, Albert Thomas. Michael Joseph, 1944.

Wonders of Ireland, Eric Newby and Diana Petry. London, 1969.

There is a story told of two village women standing outside their respective cottage
doors, conversing. A large furniture van came down past the lodges and through
the huge battered gates at the top of the village street, and lumbered towards them.
'Did you know the Poers were leaving?' 'Yes,' came the reply, 'but then we knew they
wouldn't stay long.' The Poers had come with the Norman invasion.
They left the house in the 1960s.